SOMME 1916

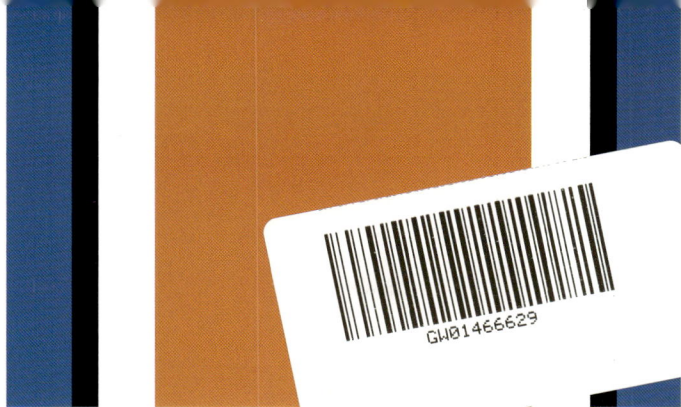

FROM DURHAM TO THE WESTERN FRONT

IN ASSOCIATION WITH THE TRUSTEES OF THE DLI COLLECTIONS

Durham County Council

Durham University

Palace Green Library

INTRODUCTION

2016 marks the centenary of one of the most infamous military engagements in British history, the Battle of the Somme. The campaign to break the stalemate that had developed in northern France involved many men and women from County Durham and it seemed fitting that their contribution – and for some, ultimate sacrifice – was marked in their home county. *Somme 1916: From Durham to the Western Front* is the story of our county's contribution to the Battle of the Somme, the name that has become embedded in our folk memory and which is synonymous with the horrors of the First World War.

Durham was used to seeing its sons march off to war. As recently as 1900 the Durham Militia had fought in the South African campaign, and in August 1914 the European conflict seemed as if it would be little different. Durham appeared well prepared with its Territorial Force close to full strength.[1] The national press announced that the war would be over by Christmas, although locally there seems to have been an understanding that it was likely to last much longer. Councillor Charles Caldcleugh, the Mayor of Durham in 1914, accepted 'the probability of the war lasting some considerable time'.[2] Support from within Durham was nonetheless strong, with civic leaders from Rabbi Sandleson[3] to Dean Henson[4] endorsing the commitment to the conflict, and community organisations enthusiastically fundraising for the war effort, including Lady Lambton who guided the coordination of comforts for the troops from

Below: Four soldiers of the 18th Battalion, The Durham Light Infantry, displaying their uniforms from right and left sides, back and front, at a camp in the United Kingdom, *c.*1914.

Above: Ravensworth Camp, near Gateshead, 1914, where the 8th Battalion, The Durham Light Infantry, was temporarily stationed.

43, North Bailey – now the University's History Department – which would ultimately result in the production of 12,500 shirts and 50,000 pairs of socks.[5] The county swiftly became an armed camp with businesses and buildings mobilised into supporting the war effort.

As the conflict extended beyond the end of 1914 it became clear that the country was engaged in total war. In the North East, from the Tyne to the Tees, the war was being fought by volunteers to the armed forces, communities, companies (contributing manpower and converting their industry to the war effort) and increasing numbers of women. No one could seemingly escape its clutches, which would ensure that the war had greater significance for Durham than any previous conflict.

---

1   Minutes of the Durham Territorial Force Association, 17 July 1914
2   *Durham Chronicle* 25 September 1914 reporting a speech in Durham Town Hall
3   *Durham Chronicle* 14 August 1914
4   *Durham Chronicle* 16 October 1914
5   Minutes of Durham County Council, 25 September 1914 and 30 January 1919

Scene from a Field Hospital, by Private Thomas McCree Scott, 2nd Battalion, The Durham Light Infantry.

Everyone knew someone who was fighting and could see the contribution of their county to the war effort: recruiting parties were out in force in every part of Durham and recruits could be seen openly being massed and trained, battalions of soldiers were being billeted in all manner of public buildings, businesses were feeling the loss in many ways, casualty lists were appearing and curtains were being drawn, buses were taking workers to the munitions factories from across Durham, commodities were becoming scarce due to their diversion to the war effort, and queuing was increasingly becoming the norm. The First World War established Durham as a martial county, a source for not just recruits but for a support for the Durham soldier that still exists today. Our exhibition offers a glimpse into what life was like for many Durham people and offers visitors the chance to reflect on the contribution and sacrifice made by so many.

The exhibition has been developed by the Culture Durham Exhibition Team, in partnership with colleagues from Durham County Record Office and the Durham Light Infantry Museum. It is the latest in our series of major summer exhibitions which began in 2013 with the hosting of the hugely successful Lindisfarne Gospels: one amazing book, one incredible journey, and includes last year's award-winning Magna Carta and the Changing Face of Revolt. These exhibitions have contributed significantly to affirming Durham's place on the cultural map, showcasing the excellent research of our academics and bringing thousands of visitors to our wonderful city.

It also sees us working with our Durham partners once again – not just our colleagues at Durham County Council and Durham Cathedral, but also the many institutions and volunteer and community organisations which together make Durham an exciting and fulfilling place to work in, and enable us to build so much more than an exhibition, with events and activities of all kinds being delivered in Durham and beyond.

Above: Soldiers of the 18th Battalion, The Durham Light Infantry, in training at Cocken Hall, County Durham, c.1914.

Opposite: Fashion Notes. This cartoon appeared in The Whizz Bang trench newspaper created by the 6th Battalion, The Durham Light Infantry, 1916.

FASHION NOTES
UGUST: 1914.

FASHION NOTES
AUGUST: 1916.

I hope that you enjoy visiting the exhibition and that, like me, you find it a meaningful testament to all those men and women from Durham whose lives were so profoundly affected by events in 1916.

Dr Keith Bartlett
Director of Culture,
Durham University

DURHAM AT THE OUTBREAK OF WAR

Bacon's map of County Durham c.1900.

YOUR KING AND COUNTRY NEED YOU

Above right: *Field Nurse in France*, sketched by Private Thomas McCree Scott, 2nd Battalion, The Durham Light Infantry.

'OUR BOY'

He's with the Wearsiders,
The boys who do or die;
He wears a khaki tunic
In the 20th D.L.I.

Copyright   Designed and Printed by Hills & Company, Sunderland

People were encouraged to aid the war effort in different capacities, both on the front and at home. Many took on fighting roles in the Army, Navy or Flying Corps. Others served in a non-fighting capacity in the Army Service Corps, including as chaplains or by providing medical services. Both men and women kept home life and industry going during the war years.

The majority of Durham men served with the Durham Light Infantry (DLI), but many others served with different regiments from across the country. Recruitment was not strictly geographical, and during the war soldiers could be transferred to other units, for example to replace casualties.

Women were also expected to do their bit. Some worked as nurses, while many took over men's jobs in factories, agriculture and the transport industry.

MICHAEL LOWERY
(1893–1916)

In 1914, Michael Joseph Lowery was one of 397 men working at Bowburn colliery when he decided to volunteer for Kitchener's New Army. In October or November he enlisted with the 25th Battalion Northumberland Fusiliers (Tyneside Irish) at 78 North Road in Durham, alongside his brothers-in-law, John and James McKeown. John and James didn't have Irish roots, but wanted to support Michael, whose mother came from Ireland.

Michael had married James' sister Eliza only a few months earlier, and had subsequently moved in with Eliza, James, John, and their parents at 22 Clarence Street in Bowburn.

Lance Corporal Michael Lowery of Bowburn, County Durham, 25th Battalion of the Northumberland Fusiliers (the Tyneside Irish Battalion).

After months of training, their battalion arrived in France in January 1916. In May, they were moved to the Somme to prepare for the upcoming battle.

When the Battle of the Somme began on 1 July 1916, Michael, John and James were three of the 3,000 Tyneside Irish soldiers who went over the top and across no man's land towards the German

Lance Corporal Michael Lowery of Bowburn, County Durham, 25th Battalion of the Northumberland Fusiliers (the Tyneside Irish Battalion).

front line at La Boiselle. Within hours, Michael and James became two of the six hundred Tyneside Irish soldiers who were killed in action. A further 1,500 soldiers from this brigade were wounded.

Michael was 23 when he died. He left behind his wife and three-month-old baby, named after him. Unfortunately, the family was not alone in their grief: Bowburn paid a steep price for its sons' war service. Neighbour Mary Hunter became a widow on the same day as Eliza. Her husband Jack Hunter was also killed on the first day of the Somme; he was shot through the head while helping a wounded soldier. By 1918, the two hundred homes in the village had lost 47 men.

Michael, James and Jack's bodies were never identified. Instead, their names are inscribed on the Thiepval Memorial to the Missing. They are three among 72,253 names on the memorial, the majority of which were killed during the Battle of the Somme.

Right: Memorial plaque presented to the family of Michael Lowery.

Below: Remembrance card: 'In loving remembrance of Lce. Corp. M.J. Lowery'.

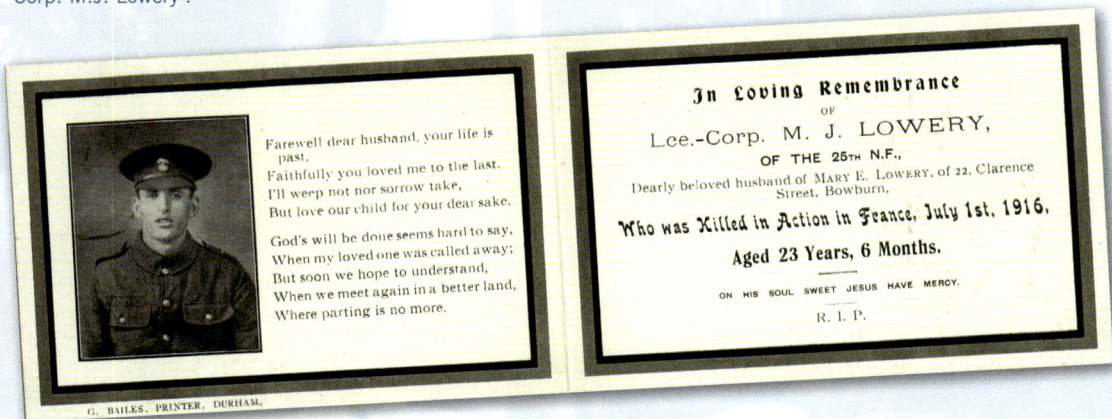

Farewell dear husband, your life is past,
Faithfully you loved me to the last,
I'll weep not nor sorrow take,
But love our child for your dear sake.

God's will be done seems hard to say,
When my loved one was called away;
But soon we hope to understand,
When we meet again in a better land,
Where parting is no more.

G. BAILES, PRINTER, DURHAM.

In Loving Remembrance
OF
Lce.-Corp. M. J. LOWERY,
OF THE 25TH N.F.,
Dearly beloved husband of MARY E. LOWERY, of 22, Clarence Street, Bowburn,
Who was Killed in Action in France, July 1st, 1916,
Aged 23 Years, 6 Months.
ON HIS SOUL SWEET JESUS HAVE MERCY.
R. I. P.

ENLIST TO-DAY!

"

All eligible men are cordially invited to join at once to fight for the great principles of freedom.

– Tyneside Irish Recruitment Poster

In 1914, the British government's call to serve for 'King, Country and Empire' had a powerful effect on British society. Recruitment drives were held in towns and cities across the country. The appeal for both soldiers and non-fighting roles was met with an enthusiastic response.

Before the war, Britain had a small standing army, consisting of full-time Regular and part-time Territorial battalions. As soon as war was declared, Lord Kitchener, the newly appointed Secretary of State for War, led a recruitment drive to enlist recruits for his New Army. Some men joined a 'Pals' battalion, like 18 DLI, so they could serve together with friends, neighbours and workmates. At the start of the war, between 75 and 100 men were enlisting in County Durham each day.

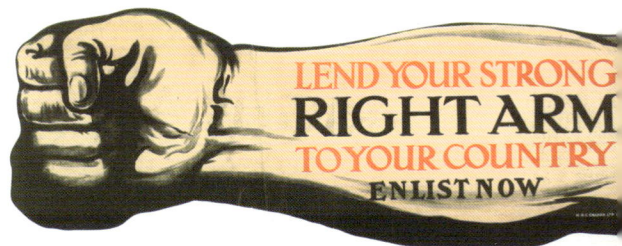

WHY AREN'T YOU IN KHAKI?

Although tens of thousands of men rushed to volunteer, others could not or would not enlist. Some men were rejected for health reasons or for not meeting physical requirements. Others in reserved occupations were required to continue their work at home. Some men chose not to sign up due to family or financial circumstances, or because of religious or political objections.

With the number of volunteers decreasing, the British government introduced conscription in January 1916. This meant that all men aged between 18 and 41 were automatically enlisted into the Army. If they felt that they had good reasons to be exempted, they needed to provide proof to the government.

Conscientious objectors – men who refused to enlist – had varying motives for doing so. Some, like the Quakers, had religious objections. Others were pacifists or believed that the political reasons for the war were not justified. Conscientious objectors were often judged severely, some spending the remainder of the war in jail.

Your King & Country URGENTLY need you
YOUNG COMMERCIAL MEN!
Join the TYNESIDE COMMERCIAL BATTALION
(KITCHENER'S ARMY)
AT ONCE.

RECRUITING OFFICES:
Newcastle—91 Grey Street, 8.30 a.m. to 7.30 p.m.
33 Sandhill - 10 a.m. to 5 p.m.
Gateshead—15 High Street, 9 a.m. to 7 p.m.
(Messrs. SNOWBALL SON & CO. LTD.) WEDNESDAYS, 9 a.m. to 1 p.m.
North Shields—42 Howard Street, 9 a.m. to 6 p.m.
(Mr. JOHN W. MEADOWS.)

GOD SAVE THE KING!

"

I could not ask others to do what I believe to be contrary to Divine Government.
– *Miner Jack Gilliland, Chester-le-Street, 1916*

I've never regretted enlisting and would do it again without a moment's hesitation.
– *Private E.R. Rosette, 1915*

FROM CIVILIANS TO SOLDIERS

Kitchener's New Army proved successful, but the training and equipping of all of these new recruits was a massive challenge. The Army could not immediately meet the increased need for uniforms and equipment. Many of the recruits had to wear their own clothes and train without modern rifles.

Below: Soldiers of the 18th Battalion, The Durham Light Infantry, in training, c.1914.

Soldiers of the 18th Battalion, The Durham Light Infantry, being fitted with uniform, [Cocken Hall], n.d. [1914–15].

The recruits were sent to camps throughout Britain to undergo training. This was intended to build up their physical fitness and confidence, instil discipline and obedience, and teach basic military skills. They had to learn to function as a unit.

It was not just soldiers who needed to be trained. Some professional nurses had received specialist training before the war, but the Voluntary Aid Detachment nurses of the Red Cross had to start from scratch. Army chaplains did not receive any training on how to fulfil their role on the Western Front until 1916.

THE JOURNEY TO THE FRONT

The first British soldiers to go to the Western Front in August 1914 were professionals, many of whom had been serving for several years. They were followed from October 1914 by Territorial battalions and later by men from Kitchener's New Army, some only first seeing a battlefield just before the start of the Battle of the Somme in July 1916.

Battalions were transported to the south coast by train, before crossing the English Channel. Once in France, they were taken nearer to the front line by train, bus, or on foot. Some took a different route. In December 1915, 18 DLI was sent to Egypt to defend the Suez Canal against the Turks. They were then sent to France and arrived on the Somme in March 1916.

> **There were tears as well as joy when we left Newcastle. There was a great shout of 'good luck!' and the flags were flying.**
>
> – *Private John Clarey, 6 DLI*

Left: Durham Railway Station, 3 September 1914. Men from Durham City left to join The Green Howards. On arrival at Richmond they were split between the various service battalions that were forming.

THE FIRST DAY: THERE WAS TO BE NO TURNING BACK

> **Chums clasped hands and said 'Cheerio', not knowing what the day held in store for them.**
>
> *– Private Harry Cruddace, 6 DLI*

The Battle of the Somme began on 1 July 1916 at 7.30am. By nightfall, 20,000 British soldiers had lost their lives, making it the bloodiest day in the history of the British Army.

This joint Anglo-French battle intended to grind down the German Army, and show that the British were playing their part. During the last week of June, the British and French artillery pounded the enemy lines. This warned the Germans that something was about to happen and they stayed in their deep dugouts until the British infantry had left their trenches to advance across no man's land.

The British infantry had been ordered not to turn back under any circumstances, resulting in many walking straight towards their deaths.

Only two DLI battalions, 15 and 18 DLI, joined the first day's attack. Combined, they lost more than 700 men to death or wounds. Many other Durham men were serving with the Tyneside Irish and Tyneside Scottish battalions of the Northumberland Fusiliers.

A support company of an assault battalion of the Tyneside Irish Brigade, going forward shortly after zero hour on 1 July 1916 during the attack on La Boisselle.

THE BATTLE CONTINUES

> **I cannot stand much more of this.
> My nerves are getting very groggy.**
>
> *– Lieutenant Rex Gee, 15 DLI*

Attack on Butte de Warlencourt, from a sketch by Lieutenant Robert Mauchlen, 9th Battalion, The Durham Light Infantry.

Although the first day of the Somme is what dominates British remembrance, this battle in fact continued for another four and a half months. It consisted of several major actions across the Somme area, some lasting for a couple of days, others for weeks. Although some ground was captured, the Germans defended doggedly and the Allies could not achieve a breakthrough.

On 5 November 1916, three DLI battalions took part in an attack on the Butte de Warlencourt, a small mound on the north-east edge of the battle area. The Butte was briefly captured by 9 DLI, but the attack ultimately failed with heavy losses. The Butte was one of the last actions of the Battle of the Somme, which formally ended two weeks later on 18 November. In total, the Allies only managed to advance five miles.

Attack on Butte.

ROLAND BOYS BRADFORD VC MC
(1892–1917)

Only two brothers were awarded the Victoria Cross during the First World War – George and Roland Bradford of Witton Park, County Durham. Roland was born in February 1892, the fourth (and youngest) son of George Bradford, a colliery manager.

In 1910, Roland Bradford joined the 5th (Territorial) Battalion DLI in Darlington, before he was commissioned in 1912 as a Regular officer in the 2nd Battalion DLI. In September 1914, 2 DLI sailed for France and within days the battalion had suffered in a few hours almost as many casualties as the entire Regiment had lost in the Boer War. In 'D' Company the only officer to survive was Roland Bradford.

In February 1915, Lieutenant Bradford was awarded the Military Cross for his bravery. Promotion soon followed and in August 1916 he was given command of the 9th Battalion DLI as a Temporary Lieutenant Colonel, even though his permanent rank was still only Lieutenant and he was only twenty-four years old.

Colonel Bradford commanded 9 DLI in September 1916 during the later stages of the Battle of the Somme and then, on 1 October during an attack at Eaucourt l'Abbaye under heavy German machine-gun fire, he took control of the 6th Battalion DLI after its commanding officer had been wounded. Then 'by his fearless energy under fire of all descriptions, and by skilful leadership of the two battalions, regardless of all danger, he succeeded in rallying the attack, captured and defended the objective, and so secured the flank' (Official citation).

For his leadership and bravery during the attack, Roland Bradford was awarded the

a former scholar of our School.

Brigadier-General. Roland Boys Bradford. V.C., M.C. Killed in France. Nov. 30. 1917.

Right: Brigadier General Roland Boys Bradford VC MC of Witton Park, County Durham.

Opposite: Roland Boys Bradford at Armentières, France, 1915.

Below: Roland Boys Bradford's Victoria Cross citation: 'For conspicuous bravery and good leadership in attack…'. Supplement to *The London Gazette*, 25 November 1916.

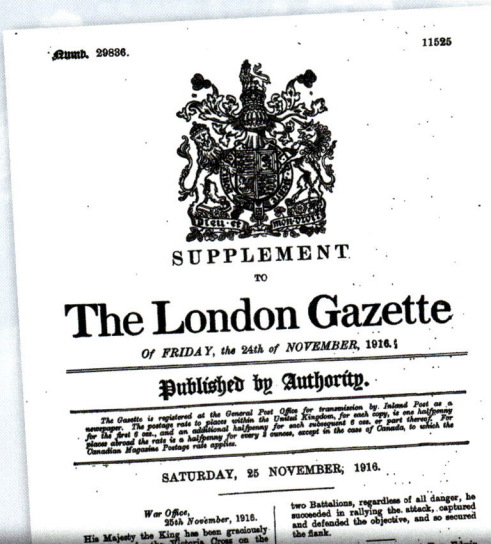

Victoria Cross, which was presented to him by King George V in June 1917. In recognition of his abilities, Colonel Bradford was promoted in early November 1917 and given command of the 186th Infantry Brigade. His career as a brigadier-general, however, lasted just 20 days, as he was killed by shell-fire on 30 November 1917. He was twenty-five years old.

In April 1918, Roland's brother, George Bradford, was awarded a posthumous Victoria Cross following the Royal Navy's raid on Zeebrugge in Belgium.

comfortable has been rent and torn away; all that is sordid and ghastly and terrible remains.

– Reverend Canon Cyril Lomax, 8 DLI

ON THE FRONT LINE

BEHIND THE LINES

Soldiers spent most of their time away from the front line. Usually battalions would spend four to six days there, followed by the same amount of time in support and reserve trenches and rest camps behind the lines.

Away from the front line the Army arranged many activities to prevent boredom and maintain discipline. Most men were young and able to recover their morale after sleep, a good meal and a bath. Concerts, football competitions and horse shows were all popular. Private soldiers would be lucky to get one week's leave per year.

Below: Football results as featured in *The Whizz Bang* trench newspaper created by the 6th Battalion, The Durham Light Infantry, 1916.

Football Results.

The results of matches played up to date were :—

6th D.L.I., 1; 7th D.L.I., 1.
6th D.L.I., 5; L.N. Lancs., 0.
6th D.L.I., 1; 8th D.L.I., 3.
6th D.L.I., 1; 9th D.L.I., 2.
6th D.L.I., 2; 7th D.L.I., 2.
6th D.L.I., 0; 8th D.L.I., 2.

Our record therefore is as follows :—

P.	W.	L.	D.	Goals for.	agst.
6	1	3	2	10	10

The platoon "knock-out" tournament ended in the triumph of 16 (Z Coy.), who beat 11 (Y Coy.) by 4 goals to 1, in spite of the vigorous vocal assistance rendered the latter by a certain officer, who threatened to dose all 16 platoon with No. 9 pills if they won. No. 11 put up a stirring fight.

Above: Books and eagerly awaited letters from home helped to pass the time. Pencil sketches by Private Thomas McCree Scott, 2nd Battalion, The Durham Light Infantry.

> ## "
> ## We are now in billets in a mining town, men all billeted with the pitmen and are as happy as if they were at home.
>
> *– Lieutenant Frederick Rees, 13 DLI*

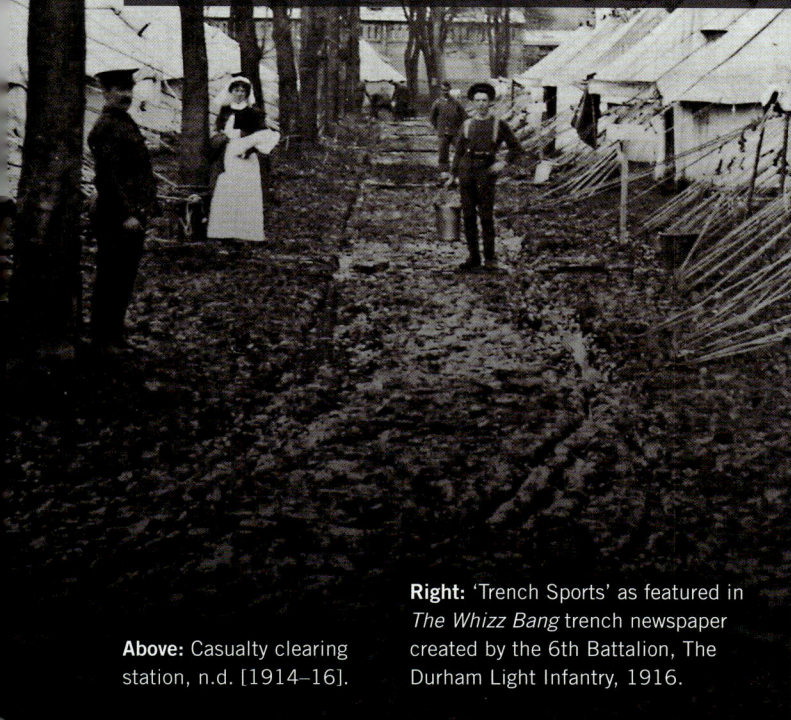

Above: Casualty clearing station, n.d. [1914–16].

Right: 'Trench Sports' as featured in *The Whizz Bang* trench newspaper created by the 6th Battalion, The Durham Light Infantry, 1916.

TRENCH SPORTS.

People in England may wonder how we in the trenches employ our spare time when " all is quiet on the Western front." Among the British, with their love of sport, many new games have sprung up, which help to while away many a tedious hour. Let me enumerate the more important of these:—

(1.) DODGING THE SAUSAGE.

This game is played between ourselves on one side and the Hun on the other. A loud explosion in your vicinity and you know the wily Bosche has kicked off. Everyone in the trench emerges from dugouts and peers eagerly at the sky, where every now and then one or more long, black missiles can be observed hurtling through the air. The object of the game is to prevent the aforesaid missile from hitting you. If it does hit you, you are immediately disqualified. Ex-cricketers used to the longfield and forgetting themselves are indifferent players. The game is made harder by groups of men who invariably stand about the trench and shout to everyone to run the wrong way and hinder anybody who tries to go the right way.

(2.) RELIEFS.

Two subalterns arrange for a dark and, if possible, wet night when the roads are being shelled, and on being relieved set out from the trenches with their respective platoons to walk (or crawl) the 8 miles to billets. The officer who gets most of his men to arrive simultaneously with himself wins. If neither arrive with any men it is a draw. This game is very difficult.

(3.) HUNTING.

A game greatly in favour among the men, the only things needed being a shirt and good eyesight.

(4.) GUMBOOTS AND CRATERS.

First obtain a large crater after it has been rained on. Put on gumboots and proceed into it alone. When you begin to sink in the thousands of feet of mud and can't get your boots out, leave them behind and run lightly back to the trench in your socks. Causes roars of laughter. From Hamage's 1/3. Post free £12 19s. 11d. (This is not a Sports Catalogue!— Ed.)

During their time off, soldiers could visit *estaminets* – a type of French or Belgian pub – and have a home-cooked meal, usually egg and chips, beer and wine. Although soldiers had some leisure time away from the front, they still had to undergo training and carry out manual labour in support of the front-line troops.

KATE MAXEY

(1876–1969)

Kate Maxey was born in Spennymoor, the youngest daughter of a shopkeeper. When she was 23 she began training as a nurse at Leeds General Infirmary. Based at this hospital was the Army's Second Northern General Hospital. In October 1914, Kate was mobilised for France with the Territorial Force Nursing Service (TFNS).

Before 1908, there was no nursing service dedicated to the volunteer army. The Regulars had the Army Medical Service, as well as the Queen Alexandra's Imperial Military Nursing Service. The nurses who joined the new service didn't receive any special training; it was felt that their normal nursing training and experience would be sufficient to work in military hospitals during times of war.

After arriving in France, Kate was based in a hospital in Rouen, before being transferred to a casualty clearing station near Ypres. In November 1915, she started working at No. 1 General Hospital in Étretat, near the Somme. She worked here throughout the Battle of the Somme, during which she was promoted to Sister and mentioned in despatches by General Sir Douglas Haig for gallant and distinguished services in the field.

Above: Sister Kate Maxey of Spennymoor, County Durham.

Left: Temporary hospital, believed to have been converted from a casino in Étretat, France, where Kate Maxey was stationed from November 1915.

Below left: Certificate awarded to Kate Maxey with the Florence Nightingale medal, 1920.

Below: Kate Maxey's identification tags.

On 21 March 1918, the Germans bombed a railway station near the casualty clearing station where Kate was Sister in charge. She sustained serious injuries, but this didn't stop her from helping a fellow wounded nurse. Her wounds meant that she had to return to England and, against her wishes, was ordered to stay there as she had served for such a prolonged period.

For her exceptional service and courage, she received both the Military Medal and the Florence Nightingale Medal, awarded in 1920 by the International Red Cross to only 50 recipients who served in the First World War.

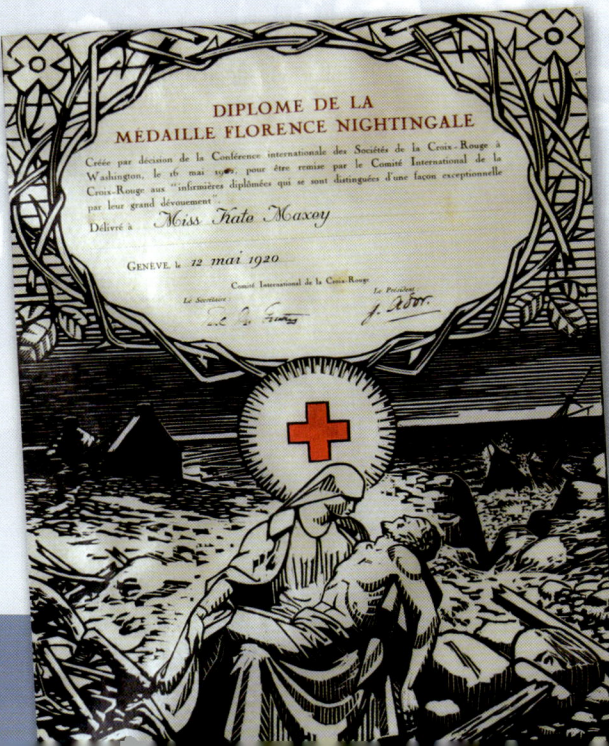

Kate Maxey remained part of the TFNS until she retired from running a nursing home in Halifax, West Yorkshire. She died in Bishop Auckland in 1969, without telling any of her surviving relatives about her war experiences.

AFTER THE SOMME

The Battle of the Somme ended on 18 November 1916, 141 days after it had begun. It was not the last or most decisive battle of the First World War, but the scale of its destruction and impact on public perception of the war has assured its continuing place in British history. More than one million people from 25 countries were killed, wounded, taken prisoner or went missing.

Though its outcome is still contested, the Battle of the Somme provided the British Army with valuable experience and improved their infantry and artillery tactics. The German Army, however, began a long decline. To avoid facing another Somme, the Germans withdrew to the Hindenburg Line. The British conducted further offensives in 1917 at Arras, Messines, Ypres and Cambrai. In 1918 the German government, with its army on the verge of disintegration and its people starving, was forced to ask for an armistice. The fighting stopped on 11 November 1918.

> " Scattered over no man's land was strewn all the wreckage of war – rifles, groundsheets, bombs, field dressings, haversacks and stretchers; and the mangled bodies of their lifeless owners.
>
> *– Sergeant Ernest Parker,*
> *10 DLI*

Durham Light Infantry memorial crosses on the Butte de Warlencourt.

FROM SOLDIERS TO CIVILIANS

The First World War had a major impact on British society, changing it forever. Many people had difficulty returning to their former lives. Around 5.5 million British men served over the span of the war; about 700,000 of those were killed, leaving millions of veterans to face the challenge of adapting to life after the war.

More than two million Britons were permanently injured. At least 80,000 men needed treatment for extreme emotional trauma with physical symptoms, known as 'shell shock'. Others never recovered from what they had seen.

During the war thousands of women had gained experience in jobs that had previously only been done by men. After the war many of these women were forced to hand over their jobs to returning soldiers. This meant giving up a better income and some newly found freedom.

Right: 18th Durham Light Infantry presenting The Colours during a homecoming parade in Durham, *c*.1919.

> What a great pity it is impossible to estimate how much the country owes to the miners for the ultimate victory, and the good-hearted manner of it.
>
> – *Private Charles Moss, 18 DLI*

SEEING IS NOT ENOUGH, ONE MUST UNDERSTAND

> "On Saturday, I took advantage of the temporary calm and had another look round Ypres. I expect the place will be flooded with sightseers and tourists after the war.
>
> – *Second Lieutenant John Gamble, 14 DLI*

Soldiers frequently brought back souvenirs, either from the battlefield or purchased in France and Belgium. These included pieces of trench art, either bought or made, and kit looted from dead or captured enemy soldiers.

In the 1920s and '30s, battlefield tourism became increasingly popular. People wanted to see where the fighting had taken place and visit the places where their loved ones had been killed. British soldiers were not repatriated, but buried in the country in which they were killed. France and Belgium gave the land for these cemeteries to the British nation.

Left: *Bound for Blighty*. Sketch by Private Thomas McCree Scott, 2nd Battalion, The Durham Light Infantry. The soldier pictured is bringing home a German Pickelhaube helmet as a souvenir.

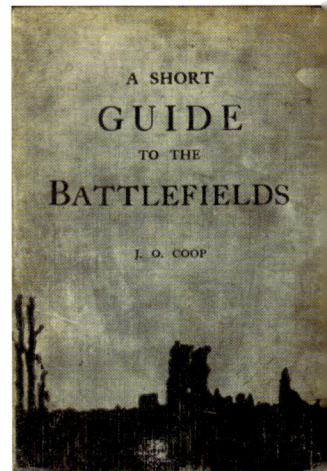

Above: Battlefield Tourism Guide, 1920.

WE WILL REMEMBER THEM

The First World War prompted a shift in how Britain remembered its fallen. It was the first war in which the majority of the British Army consisted of non-professional soldiers. The creation of the 'Pals' battalions meant that many places across the country saw high numbers of deaths during certain battles, as men both fought and died together. In County Durham, there is only one so-called 'Thankful Village' – Hunstanworth, near Consett – a place that saw all of its men return.

The focus of national remembrance was the Cenotaph in London, completed in 1920, while throughout the country most villages and towns created their own local memorials. 29,500 of Britain's dead were from the North East. Creating memorials served to ease individual grief and provided a focal point for collective mourning and commemoration, a role they still serve today.

The silk poppy, an enduring symbol of remembrance used as early as 1918 and inspired by the poppies that grew on the Western Front.

> ## It is a noble death that your son has died, and we know that the great sacrifice, which he has made in company with so many other good men, will not have been made in vain.
>
> – *Letter written to the father of Private William Glendinning, 22 DLI*

Until the day break,
and the shadows flee away.

ROBERT FEATHERSTONE WEARMOUTH

(1882–1963)

Born in 1882, in Oxhill, County Durham, Robert Featherstone Wearmouth is unusual in having served as a soldier before becoming a chaplain.

As one of six children growing up in a poor mining family, at the age of 12 he joined his father, working at the local colliery. Seven years later he enlisted in the Northumberland Fusiliers as a Private, serving in the Boer War and in the West Indies. On his return, he left the army and trained as a Primitive Methodist minister.

When the First World War broke out he immediately volunteered as a chaplain, finally receiving his commission in May 1915. He returned to the Northumberland Fusiliers and joined his men on the front line, sometimes even going over the top with them to attend to the wounded and support the dying.

During the First World War, chaplains from different branches of the Christian church provided spiritual advice and pastoral support to front-line troops and to the many soldiers who served in a supporting role. Field Marshal Haig, Commander in Chief of the British Expeditionary Force, wrote of chaplains:

'No one could do more than a chaplain to sustain morale and explain what we're fighting for. A good chaplain is as valuable as a good General.'

REV. R. F. WEARMOUTH, C.F.
In the trenches, 1915-1918.

REV. R. F. WEARMOUTH.
Chaplain to the Forces, 1915-1920.

Rev. Robert F. Wearmouth
of Oxhill, County Durham.

> ❝
> **We ought to know how others have suffered and bled that we might have life and liberty.**
>
> – *Robert Featherstone Wearmouth,*
> Pages from a Padre's Diary, *1958*

Wearmouth's account of his service, *Pages from a Padre's Diary*, was published in 1958. He recalls his time at the front, using excerpts from his journal to illustrate the varied roles of an army chaplain; from conducting services for the troops and ministering to the dying, to selling cakes and cigarettes, to giving concertina recitals. He served as a full-time army chaplain until 1920 and continued in a part-time capacity until his retirement.

After the war he continued his studies, going on to publish books on Methodism and working-class history and eventually becoming an extramural lecturer at Durham University. He died in 1963.

Above left: Black preaching scarf worn by Protestant chaplains, 1904–30.

Left: Army Chaplaincy cap badge.

THE WAR IN DURHAM

The First World War changed people's daily lives. It was the first total war, which meant that the whole nation was mobilised to contribute. Women took over the jobs that men had performed in factories and industries, often providing them with better incomes than they had had in their pre-war jobs in service or shops. People were encouraged to raise funds and save food and money to support the war effort.

Uncertainty became the norm for Durham people. Fear of invasion was widespread. Local communities came under attack as German ships and Zeppelins raided industrial areas on the north-east coast, bringing the war directly to Durham. Meanwhile, never-ending news of battles and deaths hit communities hard.

The war changed British society forever.

Best Value in Military Equipment
AT STROTHER & SON'S,
The Practical Leather Workers,
VINE PLACE, SUNDERLAND.

Strother's Patent "Tent Head" Sleeping Valise, of Best Khaki Waterproof.
Same price as ordinary—
£3 3s.
Lettering Free.

LEGGINGS, CASES, BAGS, SAM BROWN BELTS, SOLID NICKEL SPURS, Etc.   TEL 1740.

Somewhere in France

The above photograph of Durham boys in France has been received by Messrs. Trobe, Ltd., Sunderland, manufacturers of Cremona Toffee. They look happy with the boxes of sweetmeats made in their native county. Add a packet in your next parcel for your soldier boy.

WALLIS & SON,
3 & 4, Prebend Row,
DARLINGTON.
'Phone 2560.

MILITARY OUTFITS.

SERVICE SUIT	£5/5/0	Cap and Badge	10/6 & 15/-
Bedford Cord Breeches	£2/2/0	WOLSELEY VALISES	£3/7/6
GREAT COATS	£4/4/0	Kit Bags	£3/7/6
British Warm	£3/3/0	Whistle and Cord	3/9
SAM BROWNE BELTS	£2/7/6	BURBERRY (Regulation)	£3/3/0
Haversacks	8/6	Shirts	10/6 & 11/6
Great Coat Carriers	8/6	Ties	1/6 & 2/6
	Water Bottles (Aluminium)	14/-	

The Cloth used for Service Suits is either Whipcord or Super Serge.

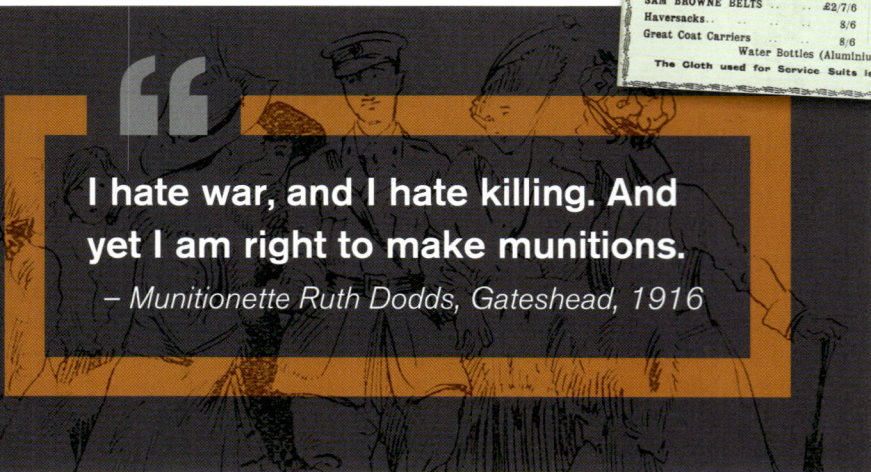

> ## "I hate war, and I hate killing. And yet I am right to make munitions.
> *– Munitionette Ruth Dodds, Gateshead, 1916*

Above: Advertisements for shops selling military supplies in County Durham placed in *The Whizz Bang*.

Opposite: *Home on Leave*, from *The Whizz Bang*, trench newspaper created by the 6th Battalion, The Durham Light Infantry, 1916.

AN IMPRESSION OF HIS FIRST LEAVE HOME FROM THE FRONT, AND

(EMBARRAS DE RICHESSE.)

HIS SECOND! (Napoo!)

PALACE
WINGATE.

Thursday, November 2nd, 1916

THE BATTLE
OF THE SOMME

The greatest battle picture ever filmed.

ONE HOUSE
Thursday and Friday, at 7-30.

THREE HOUSES
Saturday, 2-30, 7 & 9 o'clock.

Prices as usual.

NO HALF TICKETS issued on SATURDAY NIGHT.

The CHILDREN'S MATINEE will be held on Friday—**5** o'clock.

NEXT WEEK:

An American's Home

A GREAT PICTURE.

F. W. Mason, Printer, High Street, Hartlepool

D/X 313/6.

DURHAM AND *THE BATTLE OF THE SOMME* FILM

The Battle of the Somme was released in Great Britain in August 1916 and was an immediate sensation. It was shot in June and July 1916 on the battlefield by two cameramen, Benjamin McDowell and Geoffrey Malins, and presented the most brutal portrayal of war so far seen, showing the dead and wounded of both sides. Accusations of faking, made at the time by the Germans and subsequently by critics, have been proved by modern research to be almost entirely unfounded. Crucially, the film showed audiences what their loved ones in the trenches were experiencing. The film was shown for a week from Monday 25 September at both Durham cinemas, the Globe and the Assembly Rooms. The latter on that evening was 'packed to the utmost capacity' and the *Durham Chronicle* stated that for local women making medical supplies it would 'give a new meaning to their work'. Special showings were arranged for Durham School, St. Hild's College and for wounded soldiers in the neighbourhood. The film was still showing in parts of County Durham in November.

Not everybody was in favour. The Dean of Durham, Hensley Henson, wrote a letter to the *Times*, published on 1 September 1916, in which he protested at the showing of 'pictures which present the passion and death of British soldiers in the Battle of the Somme.' Despite Henson's opposition there is no evidence he ever saw the film. Soon afterwards he was invited to preach before George V at Windsor and was embarrassed to find that the King had enthusiastically endorsed the film. Henson tried to discuss his doubts with the King: 'I did manage to say that there were some things too sordid for exhibition … but His Majesty is so loquacious that it is difficult to get a word in'. The *Durham County Advertiser*, possibly referring to Henson, took a contrary view on 22 September; 'these stern pictures are good medicine. The squeamish few can stay away. The great public whose hearts are beating for their boys at the front will pack the cinema.'

Opposite: Poster for *The Battle of the Somme.*

CHRONOLOGY OF THE BATTLE OF THE SOMME

29 December 1915	General Haig, Commander in Chief of the British Expeditionary Force, attends Chantilly conference to plan a joint offensive with the French
24 June 1916	Allied bombardment commences over a 25-mile front on both sides of the River Somme
28 June 1916	Offensive postponed for two days due to bad weather
1 July 1916	Attack launched at 7.30am. Some gains in southern sector but many British units suffer very heavy losses. Casualties: British *c.*58,000; French *c.*8,000; German *c.*10,000
2 July 1916	Fricourt abandoned by Germans. 15 DLI relieved, having suffered 388 casualties
4 July 1916	La Boisselle captured. 18 DLI comes out of line at Serre with over 300 dead and wounded
9 July 1916	12 and 13 DLI take part in capture of Bailiff Wood
14 July 1916	British night attack on German second line with capture of Longueval and Bazentin-le-Petit
15 July–3 Sep 1916	Fierce fighting in Delville Wood, particularly by Scottish and South African units, to protect British right flank
29 July 1916	Australians capture Pozières
4 Aug 1916	13 DLI suffer heavy losses in attack on Munster Alley
27 Aug 1916	10 DLI capture Edge Trench in Delville Wood. 209 dead and wounded
2 Sep 1916	First Canadian troops arrive on the Somme
3 Sep 1916	British attacks in Ancre valley fail with heavy losses. 11 DLI in successful attack on Guillemont
5 Sep 1916	Allies now occupy the whole of the German second line
15 Sep 1916	First use of tanks by the British. Flers, Martinpuich, Courcelette and High Wood captured. 2, 5, 6, 8, 9, 10, 14, 15 and 20 DLI involved in operations
16 Sep 1916	Mouquet Farm captured by British. New Zealand Division gains ground near Flers
26 Sep 1916	Thiepval captured. Further south, Combles finally falls
28 Sep 1916	Schwaben Redoubt captured. German lines north of River Ancre now vulnerable
1 Oct 1916	Battles of the Ancre Heights and Transloy Ridge begin. Successful attack on Flers Line by 50 (Northumbrian) Division. Lt-Col R.B. Bradford of 1/9 DLI wins Victoria Cross at Eaucourt l'Abbaye
7 Oct 1916	12 and 13 DLI take part in the capture of Le Sars
18 Oct 1916	First frost of the winter. Weather deteriorates badly in the following weeks
5 Nov 1916	151 Brigade (1/6, 1/8 and 1/9 DLI) attack the Gird Line through thick mud and heavy machine-gun fire. 1/9 DLI capture the Butte de Warlencourt but are driven off by counter-attacks
11 Nov 1916	Canadians finally capture Regina Trench after 42 days of fighting
13 Nov 1916	Beaumont-Hamel and St. Pierre Divion captured by British. Beaucourt falls the following day. All were objectives on 1 July
18 Nov 1916	Official end of the Battle of the Somme. French hold Sailly-Saillisel and St. Pierre Vaast Wood
14 Mar–5 Apr 1917	Germans abandon Somme battlefield and withdraw to the Hindenburg Line